NATIONAL AUDIT OFFICE

REPORT BY THE
COMPTROLLER AND
AUDITOR GENERAL

Department of National Heritage, National Museums and Galleries: Quality of Service to the Public

ORDERED BY
THE HOUSE OF COMMONS
TO BE PRINTED
15 JULY 1993

LONDON : HMSO
841   £8.25 NET

This report has been prepared under Section 6 of the National Audit Act 1983 for presentation to the House of Commons in accordance with Section 9 of the Act.

John Bourn
Comptroller and Auditor General

National Audit Office
6 July 1993

The Comptroller and Auditor General is the head of the National Audit Office employing some 800 staff. He, and the NAO, are totally independent of Government. He certifies the accounts of all Government departments and a wide range of other public sector bodies; and he has statutory authority to report to Parliament on the economy, efficiency and effectiveness with which departments and other bodies have used their resources.

Contents

Summary and conclusions

1 In 1992–93 the eleven national museums and galleries in England spent about £244 million of which £192 million was granted from the Office of Arts and Libraries, now superseded by the Department of National Heritage (the Department). They attract 22 million visitors each year which represents about a quarter of all visits to UK museums and galleries. The aims of the national museums and galleries vary but all include care of collections, enabling access to the public, education and promoting enjoyment and understanding.

2 This report sets out the results of a National Audit Office examination of the quality of service to the public at the national museums and galleries. This included the planning, management and delivery of services and the effectiveness of market research and promotional services undertaken by institutions. The examination focused upon the British Museum, the National Gallery, the National Museum of Science and Industry, the Natural History Museum and the National Portrait Gallery. It also covered the role of the Department as sponsor of the national museums and galleries. The National Audit Office commissioned a survey of visitors to the museums and galleries to ascertain their opinions on the quality of service that they had received.

3 In carrying out this examination, the National Audit Office recognised the difficulties of measuring the quality of services to the public and that direct comparisons between institutions are also not always appropriate. Indeed tables of figures used in this report need to be interpreted with caution and are not intended to indicate that simple comparisons can be drawn. Each of the national museums and galleries is special and has developed its own individual style and approach to managing and delivering services. Moreover, that the National Museum of Science and Industry and the Natural History Museum charge for admission to their permanent collections while the other institutions examined do not, crucially affects the approaches adopted and has greatly focussed attention at the charging museums. Charging heightens visitors' awareness of value and quality and one would expect them to be more critical in an institution that charges. Inevitably the number of visitors at an institution is influenced by the charging policy. Consequently, measures of performance derived from visitor numbers need careful interpretation.

4 Following an arduous period of fund-raising and rebuilding, the National Portrait Gallery will open extended facilities in November 1993, enhancing many aspects of quality of service as well as aiming to achieve improvements and efficiencies for the Gallery.

On the sponsorship by the Department of National Heritage

Main findings and conclusions

5 The Department have an arms length sponsoring relationship and expect the autonomous institutions to develop their own plans, strategies and objectives for improvements in the quality of service to the public. However,

in the last five years the Office of Arts and Libraries and the Department have taken a lead and introduced initiatives to improve the organisation and management at the institutions which affect services to the public. Examples include the introduction of Corporate Plans and performance indicators and support for staff training. These are positive and worthwhile steps (paragraphs 2.2–2.3).

6 The Department meet each institution's senior management annually to discuss Corporate Plans, including financial budgets, but neither these plans nor achieved performance are used directly by the Department to determine grant levels. The relative level of grant given by the Department to each museum or gallery has not varied significantly from year to year, except for capital works or where the provision of new facilities has increased running costs. Differences in grant-in-aid per visitor in 1992–93, of between £4.20 (at the National Gallery) and £20.07 (at the Victoria and Albert Museum) mainly reflect historical funding patterns. Although the quality of Corporate Plans has steadily improved overall, institutions are not all providing the same level of planning information to the Department. Evaluation by the Department would have been aided by the issue of more specific planning guidance. The National Audit Office noted that this had been done in 1992. This should enable the Department to realise the full potential of Corporate Planning as a basis for reviewing objectives, financial forecasting and for allocating resources (paragraphs 2.4–2.8).

7 In 1992 the Department proposed new procedures whereby institutions would be required to report their achievements against their previous year's planning objectives and key indicators. The Department recognise that indicators cannot be used mechanically to compare institutions and that performance in an area such as this cannot be fully captured by quantitative indicators. The intention is for these key indicators to be used to monitor the performance of individual institutions over time (paragraphs 2.9–2.11).

On quality of service delivered to the visiting public

8 The National Audit Office examined the planning, management and review of the main services at the museums and galleries to determine the extent to which quality of service to the public and users' needs were taken into account. This included whether they had service-related objectives and how the achievement of quality of service was assessed. Findings were then compared with the results of the visitors survey commissioned by the National Audit Office. Overall, performance by institutions was good on most aspects but there was some scope for improvement as summarised in the following paragraphs. The Department are currently carrying out a study into ways in which the principles underlying the Citizens' Charter are being applied to the national and non-national museums and galleries they sponsor.

(a) Staffing and organisation

9 The National Audit Office found that there had been very significant changes in the organisational structures, staffing arrangements and training, which had been driven by concern on the part of individual institutions to improve quality of service to the public. In recent years all of the institutions examined had revised their staffing and training and had taken initiatives on contracting-out work and employing relevant professionals in commercial areas. Some institutions considered that, in former years, curatorial dominance of planning decisions had not always resulted in

priority being given to service to the public. Changes were such that institutions no longer consider this an impediment to improvements in service (paragraphs 3.2–3.3).

(b) Planning, management and review of services to the public

10 The National Audit Office recognised the importance given to quality of service at all institutions visited, and the progress made in planning, management and review of services. Quality of service was a planning priority for all of the institutions but the emphasis upon it varied. Moreover, few objectives or targets were expressed in measurable or assessable terms related to quality of service; and the information systems did not always allow the full costs of activities to be monitored and controlled (paragraphs 3.4–3.7).

11 Through visits to other organisations, external assessment and consultancy reviews, the institutions had, to varying degrees, supplemented in-house expertise when planning for quality services to the public. This enabled new ideas and perspectives on quality of service to the public to be taken on board. There were significant variations, however, in the extent of market research that institutions had carried out, with that undertaken by the National Museum of Science and Industry being considered particularly impressive by the marketing consultant engaged by the National Audit Office (paragraphs 3.8–3.13).

12 The National Audit Office consider that there would be advantages, particularly in informing management decisions, in assessing achievements and in demonstrating value for money, to be had from:

- defining service-related objectives and targets within individual institutions in terms which would allow delivered quality of service to be assessed;

- identifying the full resource costs of activities so as to inform better the decisions on allocation of resources between competing services;

- undertaking further comparisons, particularly with other major visitor attractions, when planning services;

- undertaking further visitor and non-visitor research, particularly to inform decisions on major development projects and in planning new exhibitions.

(c) Delivery of services to the public

13 The National Audit Office reviewed services under the headings of: Education; Exhibition and Display; Information and Interpretation; Widening Access; and Retailing and Catering. They considered the information used to plan the services and the measurement by institutions of their success. Findings were compared with the results of the visitor survey commissioned by the National Audit Office. Overall visitor satisfaction was high with 98 per cent of respondents to the survey being satisfied or very satisfied (paragraphs 3.14–3.15).

14 We found that many of the institutions had been very effective in tailoring their educational services and facilities to suit the emerging National Curriculum and had attracted large numbers of school visits. Satisfaction of schools and teachers with these free services was high (paragraphs 3.16–3.20).

15 New exhibitions and displays can be very costly. For example, "Dinosaurs" at the Natural History Museum cost about £3 million. All institutions take great care planning displays and exhibitions, in part because more up-to-date displays have greater appeal to the public. Refurbishment and replacement programmes could take at least 10 years and the National Museum of Science and Industry and the Natural History Museum considered that their refurbishment programme was not keeping pace with the rate of decay of their galleries, nor with the changes in science and technology. They believed that the progressive ageing of their galleries represented the most serious short comings in terms of quality of service to visitors. The National Audit Office survey suggested that the vast majority of visitors were satisfied with the exhibitions and displays. We consider it important that institutions devote sufficient resources and attention to the planning of exhibitions and displays, and particularly the heavy investment in renewal, so as to ensure that it is best directed to quality of service (paragraphs 3.21–3.26).

16 The National Audit Office noted that various modern and innovative information and interpretation devices were used to improve visitors' experiences. Examples included the British Museum's triptych information board in the main foyer, the National Gallery's interactive computer information systems, the Micro Gallery, and the Science Museum's use of drama in the galleries and "explainers" trained in communication to inform young people. However, we consider that visitor satisfaction might be further improved by more prominent display of guide books, programmes of events and floor plans and by better siting of information desks at some of the institutions. Also, the National Audit Office considered that, despite the large numbers of overseas visitors, foreign language information provision was very limited, especially at the National Portrait Gallery and the Natural History Museum (paragraphs 3.27–3.32).

17 The National Audit Office found that all institutions had widened access to the collections in a number of ways, including loans, tours and publications. But it was difficult for institutions to measure the added service to the public from such widened access. We consider that the development, refinement and monitoring of cost and of performance indicators should aid future decisions on widening access (paragraphs 3.33–3.36).

18 The hours for which institutions were open each year varied by 20 per cent and many commercial facilities, particularly contract catering, closed up to an hour before the institution. While recognising that there are cost implications, we consider that the policies on opening hours, particularly for visitor facilities, should be reviewed (paragraphs 3.37–3.38).

19 All institutions reviewed had shops and mail order arrangements, and all had catering outlets, except the National Portrait Gallery who had plans for restaurant facilities in due course. Most are run by contractors or franchisees. The National Audit Office visitor survey showed that on average only 60 per cent visit a shop. The average spend by visitors at the shops varied from 56p to 92p between the institutions and generally seemed low by industry standards for visitors attractions where £1 would be a reasonable target after allowing for school parties. Catering facilities were used by three out of ten respondents to the survey and their main criticism was of high prices. The non-acceptance of credit cards at several of the

catering outlets may be an inconvenience, particularly for overseas visitors and could well lose customers. We also consider that keeping the shops open for a short period after the museum or gallery closed would offer many visitors a chance to make purchases which would otherwise be denied. Of course the commercial, as well as service, benefits would need to be weighed against the costs of opening shops longer (paragraphs 3.39–3.45).

On promotion and public relations

20 All institutions visited were among the top visitor attractions in the UK and all actively promoted and marketed their services to the public. At both the Natural History Museum and the Science Museum, professional marketing activities had expanded rapidly since the late 1980s when admission charges were introduced. Both museums had researched non-visitors to ascertain what misconceptions, apprehensions or prejudices inhibited their potential audiences. The Science Museum advertised effectively to change some of the common misconceptions. The National Audit Office considered that there was a need for institutions regularly to determine their visitor profile so as to enhance their future planning, and for institutions to undertake further research of non-visitors, perhaps as a joint venture, to ascertain and further break down barriers against visiting (paragraphs 4.1–4.7).

21 The institutions undertook a wide range of innovative activities to promote themselves and to provide information on their collections, services and facilities. Examples included extensive publications programmes, mail order arrangements, product licensing and merchandising, in addition to advertising, press launches and more routine leafleting and listing in guide books (paragraphs 4.9–4.11).

22 In the opinion of the National Audit Office, institutions could increase the effectiveness of their promotional work by clearer identification and targeting of different visitor groups. Furthermore, they would be better placed to demonstrate the value for money of their promotional, marketing and advertising activities if they were to measure much more comprehensively the considerable costs associated with such activities, to set targets for the achievements expected and to monitor the effectiveness of their promotions, marketing and advertising. We recognise the difficulties in carrying out such assessments but note that the Science Museum had taken steps to gauge the effectiveness of their advertising and that the Natural History Museum had introduced "effectiveness of advertising" as a performance indicator for 1992–93 (paragraphs 4.12–4.15).

23 The marketing consultant engaged by the National Audit Office concluded that at each of the five institutions examined the overall standard of marketing, of customer orientation, of presentation and of delivery of the product was good by British and international standards, and at some of them it was outstanding. Further, the consultant considered that although some of the national museums and galleries have been slow to embrace new marketing ideas and techniques, all have done so to some extent at least and over the last ten to fifteen years have made great strides in becoming more attuned to the task of attracting visitors and customers. We concur with that overall assessment and suggest that each institution might benefit from emulating some of the innovative steps of the others. All might benefit from more focused attention upon visitor research and evaluation of promotional and marketing activities.

Part 1: Background and scope

Background

1.1 The eleven national museums and galleries funded by the Department of National Heritage — formerly the Office of Arts and Libraries — spent about £244 million and received government grants of over £192 million in 1992–93. The work of each is influenced by its collections, which are typically of international importance and are of inestimable value; by whether admission is free of not; by the institution's buildings, which are often national monuments in their own right; and, in some cases, by their internationally significant research work. Many of the institutions have a place at the cultural heart of the nation that attracts to them articulate and effective supporters with firm views as to the proper role of such institutions.

1.2 The aims of the national museums and gallaries vary in important respects and emphasis, but all include care of national collections, enabling access to the public, promoting enjoyment, understanding and education. The public to whom access is offered includes academics, researchers, interested amateurs, correspondents and those interested in publications and films based on the collections, as well as the ordinary visiting public. Museums and galleries are clearly conscious of a responsibility to future generations as well as to today's public.

1.3 A large proportion of the 22 million who visit the national museums and galleries do so primarily as a leisure activity. Their expectations are shaped in part by their experiences and the reputation and facilities of other leisure attractions at home and abroad. The 1970s and 1980s saw the opening of over 500 new independent museums and galleries in the United Kingdom each aiming to sustain itself on the leisure time of the general public. All the national museums and galleries acknowledge the importance of encouraging visitors and of the quality of service offered to them. They also recognise the difficulties in measuring the delivered quality of service.

1.4 In 1988 the National Audit Office and the Public Accounts Committee (HC 394 1987/88) reported upon the Management of the Collections of the English National Museums and Galleries. The individual institutions have continued their efforts to improve the conservation, storage and accessibility of their collections since that time.

Scope of National Audit Office examination

1.5 Against this background the National Audit Office reviewed arrangements that contribute to the quality of service to the visiting public at the British Museum, the National Gallery, the National Portrait Gallery, the National History Museum and the National Museum of Science and Industry. The review also included the museums at Bradford and York operated by the National Museum of Science and Industry. The National Audit Office reviewed the relationship with the Department of National Heritage (the Department) as sponsoring department, in as much as it relates to quality of service (Part 2). We also considered for the selected museums and galleries:

- the quality of service provided to the public, including planning, management and delivery (Part 3); and

- the effectiveness of the promotion and publicity of their services (Part 4).

1.6 To gain independent evidence of the quality of service to the public, the National Audit Office commissioned NOP to carry out a visitor survey in May 1992 to provide up-to-date comparative visitor opinions and statistics. Expertise and advice on market research promotion and publicity was provided to the National Audit Office by John Brown and Company who are specialist consultants in heritage marketing. We provided the full survey results and John Brown and Company's detailed findings to the institutions.

Part 2: Departmental initiatives for services to the public

Introduction

2.1 The differing aims, objectives and services of the national museums and galleries visited by the National Audit Office are shown in Appendix 1. Each has developed approaches to the planning, delivery and management of services to the public that reflects their objectives and the nature of their collections.

Sponsorship by the Department of National Heritage

2.2 The Department have arms length sponsoring relationships with the national museums and galleries. Each has their own statutory governing legislation and Boards of Trustees who set the objectives and priorities for the institution. The Department's aims include maintaining, increasing and making available the national collections. In that context, the Department seek to pursue a range of objectives in dealing with the national museums and galleries, designed to:

- enhance collections by acquisitions;

- increase public access to collections;

- encourage greater efficiency in the provision of services, in particular by
  — improving collections management and conservation;
  — promoting enhanced educational facilities in museums and galleries, especially in support of the National Curriculum;

- support the refurbishment of the buildings of the museums and galleries; and

- increase the total funds available to institutions through encouraging the development of partnerships with the private sector.

2.3 The Department expect institutions to develop their own plans, strategies and objectives for improvements in the quality of service to the public. However, in the last five years the Office of Arts and Libraries and the Department have introduced initiatives to improve the organisation and management at the institutions which affect services to the public. Examples include the introduction of Corporate Plans and performance indicators and, through the Museum Training Institute, support for the development of staff training.

Funding arrangements

2.4 Figure 1 shows the break down of grant-in-aid made or envisaged for future years. The relative amounts of grant given to each museum or gallery are not determined by reference to levels or types of services provided and are not directly related to performance. They have not varied significantly from year to year, except for capital works or where the provision of new facilities has increased running costs (Figure 2). Examples of the latter include the Tate Gallery in Liverpool and the Sainsbury Wing at the National Gallery.

Figure 1: Grant-in-Aid to all National Museums and Galleries

£ million	1990–91 outturn	1991–92 outturn	1992–93 outturn	1993–94 plans	1994–95 plans
Running costs	100	113	119	—	—
Purchase grants	9	9	9	—	—
Building and maintenance	55	59	64	—	—
Total Grant-in-Aid	164	181	192	193	196
Total less contributions in lieu of rates	—	—	190	191	194

Source: Department of National Heritage Annual Report 1993.
Note: From 1993–94 grant is not identified for separate elements.

Figure 2: Grant-in-Aid 1987–88 to 1993–94 and as a proportion of total allocations to National Museums and Galleries

	1987–88 outturn		1988–89 outturn		1989–90 outturn		1990–91 outturn		1991–92 outturn		1992–1993 estimated outturn		1993–94 plans	
	£ m	%	£ m	%	£ m	%	£ m	%	£ m	%	£ m	%	£ m	%
British Museum	13.9	16	23.6	17	24.7	17	28.0	17	31.3	17	32.4	17	34.1	18
National Gallery	7.0	8	11.2	8	12.5	9	14.4	9	16.5	9	17.9	9	17.9	9
National Museum of Science and Industry	9.6	11	16.0	11	16.7	12	18.5	11	19.7	11	22.4	12	21.9	11
National Portrait Gallery	1.9	2	5.2	4	3.8	3	4.3	3	6.2	3	5.6	3	4.8	2
Natural History Museum	18.0	20	21.7	15	21.7	15	25.3	15	27.8	15	28.9	15	28.4	15

Source: Department of National Heritage Annual Report 1993.
Note: Increases in 1988–89 reflect transfers of responsibility for building expenditure. Increases in 1991–92 reflect new arrangements for the payment of contributions in lieu of rates.

2.5 The Department encourage institutions to raise additional income to supplement their grant so as to provide improved services to the public. All institutions actively seek sponsorship, mainly for specific building works, refurbishments or new exhibitions. From 1987 the Office of Arts and Libraries allowed institutions to retain such receipts without affecting their grants, so as to provide an incentive to extend and improve their trading activities. Self-generated income now amounts to about £52.4 million or 27 per cent of grant-in-aid in 1992–93 (Figure 3).

2.6 Differences in grant-in-aid per visitor of between £4.20 and £23.20 are in small part due to different treatment of categories of income and are influenced by inaccuracies in some visitor numbers as described in paragraph 2.10. But underlying differences are large and reflect historical funding patterns. The National Audit Office considered that institutions could usefully identify separately the costs associated with visitor services so as to provide more meaningful statistics to inform decisions on visitor services. We recognise that some costs cannot easily be separated, but consider that pragmatic and consistent cost attribution could contribute to improved information upon which management could base decisions.

Corporate Planning and performance indicators

2.7 Since 1988 the Office of Arts and Libraries and the Department have required institutions to produce annual Corporate Plans which should provide a good planning mechanism for institutions and identify their priorities and budgets for the following five years. The Department issue formal guidance on the form and content of these plans.

Figure 3: National Museums and Galleries — Total Funding 1992/93 — Estimated outturn

	Grant-in-Aid £ m	Self Generated Income £ m	Total Income £ m	Self Generated Income as % Total Income	Grant-in-Aid per Visitor (1991 Attendances) £
British Museum	32.4	7.0	39.4	17.8	4.8
Imperial War Museum*	11.0	7.2	18.2	39.6	10.0
National Gallery	17.9	9.7	27.6	35.1	4.2
National Maritime Museum*	11.6	1.8	13.4	13.4	23.2
National Museums and Galleries on Merseyside*	13.4	0.7	14.1	5.0	11.2
National Museum of Science and Industry*	22.4	3.9	26.3	14.8	8.6
National Portrait Gallery	5.6	5.2	10.8	48.1	7.0
Natural History Museum*	28.9	9.3	38.2	24.3	18.1
Tate Gallery	16.6	3.3	19.9	16.6	7.6
Victoria and Albert Museum	30.1	3.9	34.0	11.5	20.1
Wallace Collection	1.9	0.2	2.1	9.5	9.5
Total	191.8	52.2	244.0	21.4	8.4

Source: Department of National Heritage Annual Report 1993.
*An admission charge is made. At the National Museums and Galleries on Merseyside this refers to the Maritime Museum only.

2.8 Although the quality of these Corporate Plans has steadily improved overall, institutions are not all providing the same levels of planning information or detail to the Department, and the Plans of individual institutions cannot easily be compared. Institutions recognise that an important purpose of these Plans is to outline their financial budgets and many other aspects of their work. The Department meet each institution's senior management once a year for discussion and clarification of their Corporate Plan. However, the Plans are not scrutinised at the level of individual departmental objectives. The Department makes the annual allocations to the institutions on the strength of the information contained in each Corporate Plan, taking account of the priorities of the particular institutions measured against the overall Departmental resources available and competing claims from other Departmental museums and galleries.

2.9 In late 1992 the Department proposed new procedures whereby institutions would be required, as part of the Corporate Planning process, to report their achievements against their previous year's objectives and key indicators. The Office of Arts and Libraries in 1990 used consultants, Coopers and Lybrand, to develop specific performance indicators for, and with institutions. They identified 39 quantitative and qualitative indicators. Appendix 2 shows Group 1 indicators that are for Departmental and institutional use and are required to be included in annual Corporate Plans. Appendix 3 shows Group 2 indicators which are intended for institutional use, without being disclosed to the Department.

2.10 As there are no consistent formulae for calculating each indicator, the National Audit Office were unable directly to compare measures at individual institutions (see Figure 4). Also, the National Audit Office noted that the accuracy of some indicators relied upon visitor attendance figures. Those institutions charging admission have

Figure 4: 1991–92 Performance Indicators related to quality of service, as notified to the Department

Performance Component	Measure		British Museum	National Gallery	National Museum of Science and Industry	National Portrait Gallery	Natural History Museum
Access and Use	**Movements in visitors numbers**				Science Museum +6%		
	Gallery visitors (change on previous year)		+7% (1991)	+15% (1991)	NRM −6% NMPFT +12%	NPG −1% Outstations +4%	−8%
	Educational Groups (change on previous year)		School/student parties +65% (90–1 academic yr)	Booked parties +3%	Parties −9%	Education +31%	School parties +0%
	Visitors and enquiries: library, curatorial, information		No prior year data notified to Dept.	No prior year data notified to Dept.	+8%	Researchers +0%	Visitors to departments: no change on prior year data notified to Dept.
	Visitors per sq m		273	not reported	43 (Science Museum)	242	81
	Expenditure per user: (as reported by the institution)	Gross	£6.83	not reported	£8.70	£8.08	£24.90
		Net of related income	£5.43 (excludes acquisitions)	£3.90	£7.88	£6.30	£18.82
	New Loans of items by the institution		2824	98	587	63	not reported
Visitor Care/ Display	**Visitor Satisfaction**		not reported	89% ''enjoyed or much enjoyed'' (1990)	97% ''very/fairly satisfied'' (Science M, 1991) 94% (NRM, 1991)	not reported	''High level of satisfaction'' (Ecology gallery, 1991)
	Gallery availability		95.6%	100% (excludes pre-planned closures)	99.2% (Science M) 99.9% (NMPFT)	96%	100% (excludes pre-planned closures)
Access/Display/ Visitor Care	**Visitor flow** (highest: lowest month)		not reported	2.18 (1991) (affected by opening of Sainsbury Wing)	2.48 (Science M) 6.65 (NRM) 2.7 (NMPFT)	1.4	2.8

Source: Institutions' Corporate Plans.
Note: NRM is the National Railway Museum at York.
*   NMPFT is the National Museum of Photography, Film and Theatre at Bradford.*

independent verification of attendances. Visitors to the British Museum, the National Gallery and the National Portrait Gallery are handcounted by warders, with little validation work to test the reliability of this method, although fire safety consultants' counts bear comparison with the British Museum's own figures. The Science and Natural History Museums found that automated ticketing, since 1987 and 1988 respectively, had proved that the handcounting used previously was inaccurate, in some instances recording fifty per cent more than the now known capacity. Attendance figures and derived indicators must therefore be treated with some caution.

2.11   Institutions believe that the different characteristics of each mean that, while these performance indicators will be useful to measure changes in individual institutions' performance over time, they cannot be used to compare institutions. The Department emphasised that they did not intend the indicators to be used mechanically to compare institutions but to reflect the performance of individual institutions and particularly on those aspects that individual institutions choose to emphasise. Furthermore, the Department considered that performance in an area such as this cannot be fully captured by quantitative indicators. The 1992 Office of Arts and Libraries' report stated that "it will be a further year or more before comprehensive information based on these indicators becomes available". The National Audit Office found that in 1992 the Department had not yet assessed in depth such performance indicator data as had been submitted by the institutions and were still considering the use to which the data would be put in future.

Museum Training Institute

2.12   Standards of training at the national museums and galleries were recognised by the Office of Arts and Libraries in 1987 as an area requiring improvement, and training was seen as contributing indirectly to quality of service to the public. The Office of Arts and Libraries and the Department have therefore provided the Museum Training Institute with around £400,000 per year since its establishment in 1989. The Institute's work has concentrated on introducing a qualifications framework of standards of competence for all categories of museum work which is expected to be in place by 1994. The Institute does not provide training; museums and galleries are free to provide in-house, or to contract in, training services from any of several providers to meet their particular needs.

The Museums and Galleries Commission

2.13   The Museums and Galleries Commission, funded by the Department to the extent of £8.8 million in 1992–93, is a government advisory body. They adminster grants to local authority and independent charitable museums, provide advice to museums, and develop standards. In 1992, in parallel with the National Audit Office study, the Commission developed Guidelines on Customer Care for museums and galleries based to some extent on the English Tourist Board's National Code of Practice for Visitor Attractions (1992). These were launched in December 1992, but it is too early to tell how well they have been received, or what impact they will have.

Part 3: Quality of service provided to the visiting public

3.1 The National Audit Office examined the planning, management and review of the main services at the museums and galleries to determine the extent to which quality of service to the public and users' needs were taken into account; whether they had service-related objectives; and how the achievement of quality of service was assessed. Findings were then compared with the results of the visitors survey commissioned by the National Audit Office. Overall, institutions showed up well on most aspects but there was some scope for improvement.

Staffing and organisation

3.2 The National Audit Office recognised that each institution is unique and found that the different approaches adopted to services to the public were reflected in the staffing and organisational arrangement at the institutions. All considered that their structures had been modified as necessary to facilitate good services to the public, some having undergone major reorganisation to replace the traditional curatorial hierarchy. At some museums the changes have been sweeping, for example:

> The Science Museum underwent major restructuring in the late 1980s and subsequently established a Public Affairs Division in 1992 whose primary responsibilities included "understanding and satisfying customers' needs through attention to the planning, delivery and monitoring of services".

> The Natural History Museum introduced centralised "front of house" services to the public in 1989 to ensure clear management responsibilities and facilitate coordination and monitoring of all relevant activities.

> The British Museum underwent major restructuring in the 1970s, setting up a Public Services Department in 1973. British Museum Publications Ltd. was also set up in 1973 to run the publishing and retailing operations on a commercial, customer-orientated basis.

> Public relations and press departments have been strengthened at the other institutions in recent years, although some of the traditional decision-making process had been retained. For instance, at the British Museum, each department was still responsible for most services within its subject area, including mounting exhibitions, displaying their collections, and library and research facilities.

3.3 All of the institutions had revised staffing and training arrangements so as to ease improvements in the quality of service to the visiting public. For example, departure from Civil Service pay and conditions of service; contracting-out or franchising of commercial operations; employment of relevant professionals, rather than academic staff, in commercial areas; use of freelance designers; introduction of performance appraisal and development of performance related pay; and giving basic, and more specialised, customer care training.

Planning, management and review

3.4 The institutions' Corporate Planning, as described in Part 2, is the main mechanism for review of activities and amendment of future plans and targets. Within institutions regular management meetings monitor and review activities from day to day with Trustees playing a broader supervisory and policy role, including publication of annual or triennial reviews.

3.5 The National Audit Office found that each institution had objectives for the achievement of their fundamental aims or mission (Appendix 1), including objectives for most individual departments or activities. Quality of service was a planning priority for all the institutions but the formalised emphasis upon it varied: for instance, the Science Museum had a Public Affairs Division focussing on the needs of customers; the National Portrait Gallery specified service-related objectives for each activity; and although the British Museum did not formalise their quality of service planning in these terms, most of their activities contributed to service to customers.

3.6 Institutions had some detailed service targets such as exhibition programmes for 3–5 years ahead, target dates for introducing facilities and target levels of activity. However, few objectives or targets were expressed in measurable or assessable terms related to quality of service.

3.7 The National Audit Office found that information systems at institutions did not allow monitoring and control of the full costs of activities, except for commercial activities. Service managers could generally control only direct non-staff costs and overall activity levels were fixed by the planning process. Decisions on the allocation of resources at the margin could not in most cases be related to their likely impact on service provision in any quantifiable way. Scope for corrective action when targets were not achieved was similarly limited.

3.8 Through visits to other organisations, some of the institutions had brought to their planning new ideas and perspectives on quality of service to the public. Examples included:

> at the National Gallery, planning and organisation of temporary exhibitions in the Sainsbury Wing was informed by research in American and various British art galleries. This helped the design of a pre-booking and queuing system to maximise attendances and minimise waiting times;

> the Science Museum had introduced an Interpretation Unit to improve exhibitions, based on principles used at the Smithsonian Institution. The Science Museum had also studied alternative approaches to warding at the Louvre;

> the Natural History Museum had studied approaches of American museums to commerce and marketing; and

> some institutions had sent staff on training courses on customer care provided by the Disney Corporation in the United States.

3.9 The National Audit Office found that institutions had used external reviews to supplement in-house expertise. For instance, following an internal project to improve visitor services, consultants had reviewed "front of house" management at the Science Museum. The consultants also helped develop the skills to manage, plan and deliver services. External assessors had helped plan specific galleries and displays at the Natural History Museum and the Science Museum. Consultants had recently reviewed the retail activities at the Natural History Museum. Similar reviews at the British Museum shops in 1975 and 1984 had been aimed at maximising retail turnover. Most museums contracted out some exhibition design work to achieve variety in appearance, high standards of creativity and cost-effectiveness.

3.10 To provide quality services and meet requirements of visitors, institutions need to ascertain who their visitors are, and what are their needs, attitudes and exectations. The Department emphasised the importance of supplementing the experience and professional judgements of curators' and museum managers on matters of display and services, with structured visitor research. Measurement of visitor satisfaction by opinion survey was one of the performance indicators to be reported annually to the Department.

3.11 The National Audit Office noted variations in the amount and type of visitor research carried out (Figure 5). Since 1975 the Natural History Museum has had a systematic

Figure 5: Major Visitor Surveys carried out by National Museums and Galleries in the last five years

British Museum	A two part exit and entry survey carried out in 1988, to ascertain reasons for visiting, demographic profile of visitors, usage of facilities and satisfaction. Museum of Mankind student/school group survey by SRU Ltd. in 1988. Three other focus group surveys in 1991–92. Further general visitor survey commissioned June 1992.
National Gallery	A "snapshot" survey of visitors in 1990 prior to opening of Sainsbury Wing determined the main categories of visitor, reasons for visiting, awareness of the Gallery, experiences of the visit, attitudes to facilities including shops and restaurant. Surveys have been taken of visitors responses to major exhibitions held in the Sainsbury Wing since its opening in 1991.
National Museum of Science and Industry	Science Museum—Six visitor surveys National Railway Museum—Two visitor surveys National Museum of Photography, Film and TV—Five annual visitor surveys on satisfaction and attitudes to the Museum. Focus Group work at all sites.
National Portrait Gallery	No general visitor surveys undertaken during this period. A visitor survey was carried out in 1985, and one since the National Audit Office Survey in 1992. The Gallery now plan to conduct a survey every year.
Natural History Museum	In-house visitor surveys carried out in 1991 which concentrated on demographic profile of visitors and opinions on aspects of the Museum. Externally commissioned Visitor Survey and Focus Groups on the Geological Museum prior to amalgamation in 1989.

programme for its exhibition planning based upon research into audience needs and expectations and regular evaluation after exhibitions are opened. This approach was first published in 1982 in a now internationally used handbook by the Head of the Museum's Exhibition Department— "The Design of Educational Exhibits". The Natural History Museum and the National Museum of Science and Industry had carried out extensive market research using external consultants to conduct regular visitor surveys, and smaller focus group work where chosen groups of people are led through a structured discussion as a means of assessing visitor preferences and needs. The marketing consultant engaged by the National Audit Office considered that this programme of research at the National Museum of Science and Industry was particularly impressive and that few, if any, of the major commercial attractions researched their customers as thoroughly.

3.12 The British Museum produced two manuals which form the basis of the approach to exhibition planning. Both were based on research on the way visitors use displays. The Science Museum's specialised Interpretation Unit researches and evaluates exhibitions and major projects. The total costs of the Unit in 1991–92 was £350,000 including salaries. As at the Natural History Museum, planning included identifying specific target audiences, setting objectives covering educational and other needs and input from potential visitors from the earliest planning stages. Examples of the impact of research included alteration to the

interactive "Launch Pad" exhibits at the Science Museum after trials showed that children did not use them as expected. Similarly, at the Natural History Museum, the Hall of Human Biology which was first opened in 1977, has been substantially revised to maintain its scientific coverage and relevance to educational needs.

3.13 The National Audit Office noted that more research had been undertaken for the development of the new education centre at the National Museum of Science and Industry. While little visitor or non-visitor research had been carried out relating to the National Portrait Gallery Development Plan the various elements were self evident necessities. We consider that such research has an important part to play in all significant developments and expansions by museums and galleries.

Delivery of services to the public

3.14 The National Audit Office reviewed the quality of service to the public under the headings of: Education; Exhibition and Display; Information and Interpretation; Widening Access; and Retailing and Catering. These represent the principal common services and facilities, as summarised in Appendix 4. The review considered the information used to plan the services, and the institutions' own measurement of their success. Where possible, findings were compared with the results of the National Opinion Poll visitor survey, which had been commisioned by the National Audit Office, to give an independent measure of the quality

Figure 6: Overall Visitor Satisfaction

Percentages	Total	British Museum	National Gallery	National Portrait Gallery	Natural History Museum*	Science Museum*
Very satisfied	78	79	83	74	79	69
Fairly satisfied	20	19	16	24	19	28
Neither	1	1	1	2	2	2
Fairly dissatisfied	1	1	0	0	0	1
Very dissatisfied	0	0	0	0	0	0

Source: NOP Visitor Survey prepared for NAO May/June 1992.
*Admission charge is made

of the service. An example of the questionnaire is at Appendix 5 and shows survey information.

3.15 For the general visiting public, the National Audit Office survey showed that overall satisfaction was very high, with 78 per cent of respondents being very satisfied and 20 per cent fairly satisfied (Figure 6). Noting the marginally lower levels of satisfaction at the Science Museum (69 per cent very satisfied), the Museum considered that charging heightens people's awareness of value and quality and one would expect them to be more critical in a museum that charges. The Science Museum also considered that the absence of a major programme of temporary exhibitions had an adverse effect. The Science Museum also noted that their own MORI polls conducted at five times from September 1988 to May 1992, showed more consistent and favourable results in the areas studied than those produced by the National Audit Office survey.

Education

3.16 All institutions had education departments providing special services, and access for school groups was encouraged to fulfil their educational roles and to strengthen and widen the institutions' visitor base. All the institutions provided free education services for schools and ran public lectures, guided tours and special events for adults. Figure 7 indicates the extent of education provision.

3.17 All of the museums were increasingly in demand from schools as a result of the National Curriculum. The British Museum told the National Audit Office that numbers had almost doubled in two years. The Museum had been active with the National Curriculum Council so that areas where their collections were strong became key topics in the history curriculum. The other museums had been less pro-active but considered that their collections contributed to syllabuses such as history, science or art. All institutions were developing courses or materials linked to the National Curriculum and teachers' demands.

3.18 The Science Museum, the Natural History Museum and the National Portrait Gallery had introduced measures to manage demand for educational provision because it exceeded gallery capacity. The Natural History Museum, the Science Museum and the British Museum concentrated on providing resources and advice for teachers rather than direct teaching and all museums ran classes or study days for teacher training. The National Gallery and the National Portrait Gallery concentrated more on direct teaching

Figure 7: Extent of Education Provision

	British Museum	National Gallery	National Portrait Gallery	Natural History Museum	Science Museum (1)
1992–93 Education budget (£000)	365	580	161	767	623
No of Educational users 1991–92: 000's					
school children (4)	115(2)	63(3)	15	171	237
others	46	60(3)	16	5	26
% of total visitors	3.0	2.8	3.8	11.9	20.5

Source: Corporate Plans and reports on performance indicators.
Note: (1) South Kensington site only
(2) Pre-booked groups only. Unbooked school visits may account for up to 100,000 other visitors.
(3) Estimates based on number of groups and lectures.
(4) At some museums the physical capacity restricts school numbers.

These figures are indicative of the scale of operations and are not intended to be used for comparative purposes.

to educational groups. The National Gallery and the National Portrait Gallery offered talks tailored to groups' individual requirements.

3.19 Some special facilities were geared to requirements of schools such as separate reception and lunch areas, interactive galleries at the Science Museum and a permanent and touring hands-on Discovery Centre at the Natural History Museum. The British Museum, the Science Museum and the National Portrait Gallery were anticipating increased demand and were planning new education centres with improved accommodation and more comprehensive facilities.

3.20 Institutions monitored regularly and carefully the perceptions of schools and teachers, and used this information in future plans. Overall satisfaction of schools and teachers was high. School parties were excluded from the National Audit Office's own visitor survey for legal and logistical reasons and their opinions were not sought directly.

Exhibitions and display

3.21 Display of their collections is, of course, a fundamental purpose of the institutions embodied in their aims and objectives. However, only parts of some of the collections are suitable for permanent or even temporary display. The exception is the National Gallery who usually show their complete collection including new acquisitions.

3.22 New displays and exhibitions can be costly. For example, "Dinosaurs" at the Natural History Museum cost about £3 million. All institutions take great care when planning displays and exhibitions. Generally, this is undertaken by special project teams or committees. The National Audit Office noted that rolling programmes of exhibition replacement and renewal could take at least 10 years at all institutions and up to 50 years at the British Museum.

3.23 The Natural History Museum and the National Museum of Science and Industry considered that their refurbishment programme was not keeping pace with the rate of decay of their galleries, nor with the changes in science and technology. They believed that the progressive ageing of their galleries represented the most serious shortcomings in terms of quality of service to visitors.

3.24 Temporary and special exhibitions were used to supplement the permanent displays. For the National Portrait Gallery they were important for attracting visitors as well as, in some cases, illustrating parts of the collection poorly represented in the permanent displays. The National Gallery and the British Museum used exhibitions to illustrate scholarly work at the museum and to exhibit loaned items otherwise not accessible to the public, as well as to attract visitors. Sponsorship and/or entrance charges contributed towards the direct costs of most special exhibitions; the Science Museum required a percentage of proposed new exhibition costs to be sponsored, and the Natural History Museum require all temporary exhibitions to be fully sponsored.

3.25 The National Audit Office visitor survey indicated that the more up to date exhibits had the greater appeal and those that had been carefully researched before introduction, such as "Dinosaurs" and "Creepy Crawlies" at the Natural History Museum, were particularly well received. The visitor survey suggested that the vast majority of visitors—over 96 per cent—were satisfied with the exhibitions and displays they had seen that day, including three quarters who were very satisfied.

3.26 Given that replacement and renewal of exhibitions and displays were the main ways in which institutions maintained the fabric of their collections and modernised presentation, the National Audit Office considered it important that institutions devote sufficient resources and attention to the planning of exhibitions and displays, and particularly the heavy investment in renewal, so as to ensure that it is best directed to quality of service.

Information and interpretation

3.27 To promote understanding and appreciation, all of the institutions provided visitors with interpretative information about the displays. Examples of modern and innovative approaches included:

the British Museum used a "triptych" information board, in the main foyer, showing the location of galleries, those temporarily closed and events of the day, such as talks or films;

Figure 8: Finding the way round the Museums and Galleries

Percentage use of sources of information	Floor Plan	Information Boards	Signposting	Asking Staff
British Museum	56	58	64	45
National Gallery	47	46	59	25
National Portrait Gallery	22	49	42	22
Natural History Museum	79	66	73	30
Science Museum	67	69	75	29
Total Using	57	57	65	33
Of those using, percentage finding very helpful	60	50	48	83

Source: NOP Visitor Survey for NAO prepared May/June 1992

the National Gallery's interactive computer information system, the Micro Gallery;

the Natural History Museum, in 1992, reviewed information provision, improved signage and information and revised the flow of visitors through the museum;

the synopsis gallery at the Science Museum introduced new visitors to the collections and helped them to plan their time. The Museum also used guides, drama in the galleries and "explainers" trained in communication to inform young people about the exhibitions. The Museum's Interpretation Unit worked to improve communication of scientific and technical ideas in the displays, taking into account visitors' expectations, knowledge and reactions to the content of displays;

the National Gallery had rearranged their whole collection since the opening of the Sainsbury Wing to provide a more coherent layout. They also provided free guided tours, videos and some recorded tours. The innovative Micro Gallery, which opened in 1991, allowed visitors to see on computer screens illustrations of, and information about, every picture in the collection.

3.28 Each institutution made available a floor plan in English and 60 per cent of surveyed visitors used one. Usage was very high at the Science and Natural History museums, where plans were handed out with entry tickets, but was lower at the other institutions. The National Audit Office survey indicated that other information guides and leaflets, some of which were free, were used by fewer visitors. Only one in eight picked up a programme of events, whilst only one in twelve bought a guide book. The survey showed that, of those who collected neither, 12 per cent would have liked a guide book and 11 per cent a programme of events. More prominent displays of these items might improve visitor satisfaction, as well as increasing revenue from sales of guide books.

3.29 Figure 8 shows that asking staff for directions was found to be very helpful by 83 per cent of those who asked. This highlighted the importance of customer care skills and training for staff. Since 1989, the Natural History Museum have had an extensive training programme for all the "front of house" staff in customer care and knowledge of the Museum's exhibitions. The Science Museum pointed out that they were in the middle of replacing their internal signage in May 1992, at the time of the survey, and would have expected more favourable responses later in the year. The British Museum considered that, because of their complex layout and the number of galleries, all sources of information have to be considered in measuring their effectiveness.

3.30 The National Audit Office found that access for the disabled existed at all of the museums and galleries. All take very seriously provision for the disabled when planning services and facilities. Staff are only too willing to help disabled visitors and are trained to do so. In 1992 the National Gallery received the Annual Arts Access award from the National Association for Improving Access for Disabled People. The Science Museum train "front of house" staff to help and offer wheelchairs to those who might need them. Provision for the disabled is highlighted by all institutions in their publicity material. The nature and layout of their old buildings inevitably present access problems, however, and necessitate special entrance arrangements for the disabled at some museums and galleries. The National Portrait Gallery has made disabled access a paramount concern within the Development Plan.

3.31 In addition to the survey, the National Audit Office's own review of facilities showed that not all institutions produced leaflets identifying highlights of the collections for visitors short of time; and that foreign language provision was very limited, especially at the National Portrait Gallery and the Natural History Museum, despite over one third of visitors being from overseas. Of these a high proportion will have a good command of English but significant numbers will not.

3.32 The National Audit Office considered that there was some scope for improvement, particularly in catering for the needs of visitors without command of English. The National Portrait Gallery planned to produce foreign language guides in early 1993 and were actively seeking sponsorship for them. Overall, all of the institutions had achieved good levels of satisfaction.

Widening access

3.33 Each of the institutions reviewed was enthusiastic to widen access to their collections by lending exhibits, facilitating access to reserve collections, addressing specialist interests in parts of the collections, maximising opportunities for the public to visit and through publications. All the institutions have their main collections based in London. The National Museum of Science and Industry also run the National Railway Museum at York and the National Museum of Photography, Film and Television at Bradford, both displaying specialist exhibits. The National Portrait Gallery and the Natural History Museum exhibit parts of their collections permanently at outstations. The National Portrait Gallery also have 3–4 touring exhibitions a year and the British Museum have regular touring programmes, averaging four or five a year. The National

Gallery are also developing touring exhibitions. All lend objects or paintings, particularly to other museums and galleries. For example, the Natural History Museum make an average of 50,000 specimen loans each year to other museums and research institutions around the world.

3.34 All of the institutions provided access on request to items not on display, libraries and facilities for research, and answer public and academic enquiries, in person and by correspondence, all without charge. For example, the British Museum deal with some 300,000 each year. Access to the expert knowledge of curators, scientists and others at the institutions undoubtedly played an important part in the maintenance of the reputation and prominence of the institutions in the eyes of the international institutions and others that used such services.

3.35 Publication of books and catalogues played a crucial role in disseminating knowledge of the collections and of the results of scholarship based on them. Publications also generated significant revenues. The British Museum publications turnover was almost £2 million in 1991–92. Turnover in publications at the other museums and the National Gallery was about £$\frac{1}{2}$ million in each case, the National Portrait Gallery a little less. The British Museum had led in developing a range of publications aimed at different audiences worldwide, and the National Gallery were widening their range of titles in this way. Both the British Museum and the National Gallery had partnership arrangements with distributors and the former also used joint imprinting, book clubs and selected agents to increase circulation. Networks of agents were also used by the National Portrait Gallery. The Natural History Museum and Science Museum use directly employed distribution staff. The publications from one institution can often be found in the bookshop of another.

3.36 The National Audit Office noted that it was difficult for institutions to measure the added service to the public by initiatives to widen access, other than by simple user numbers, and even that was not always possible. But the further development, refinement and monitoring of costs and performance indicators should aid future decisions on widening access. As only the general visiting public were interviewed, the National Audit

Figure 9: Opening times

		British Museum	National Gallery	National Portrait Gallery	Natural History Museum	Science Museum
Opening hours	Mon-Fri	10-5	10-6	10-5	10-6	10-6
	Sat	10-5	10-6	10-6	10-6	10-6
	Sun	2.30-6	2-6 to 8 pm on 9 Weds in Summer	2-6	11-6	11-6
Days open in 1992		358	359	359	360	362
Hours open in 1992		2328	2682	2408	2828	2844
Public Holidays Open:*						
New Year's Day		No	No	No	No	Yes
Good Friday		No	No	No	Yes	Yes
May Day		No	No	No	Yes	Yes

Source: Institutions' Information and Publicity.
All were open on Easter Monday, Spring and August Bank holidays. All were closed on Christmas Day, Christmas Eve and Boxing Day. The Natural History Museum was also closed on 23 December and the British Museum was closed on 27 December.

The Number of Days open to the public ranged from 358 to 362 and the number of hours from 2328 to 2844.

Office visitor survey did not assess the quality of service given by the various initiatives to broaden access.

Opening times

3.37 Figure 9 shows opening times for the institutions. The British Museum have opened on Sunday afternoons for a century. In recent times the Science Museum were the first to open all day on Sundays, Good Friday, Mayday and New Year's Day and were open for the most days each year. Figure 9 also shows a 20 per cent variation in the hours open each year. The National Portrait Gallery intend to extend opening hours from November 1993 when their new galleries and facilities open. While recognising that there are significant cost implications, we consider that there may be potential for some institutions to open on more public holidays as it is on such days that the public are most able to visit.

3.38 The National Audit Office visitor survey showed general satisfaction with opening hours, although the British Museum was rated lower than the other institutions. The Museum considered that this may have been due to a variety of factors, such as high visitor numbers, their popular exhibits, or the present restricted internal circulation. The National Audit Office considered that this could also be due to the normal closing time of 5 pm which is generally one hour earlier than most of the other national museums and galleries. Although not included in the survey, we observed that many commercial facilities at the institutions reviewed, particularly contract catering, closed up to an hour before the institution; and, for security reasons, some toilet facilities were also closed towards the end of the day.

Retailing and catering

3.39 All of the museums and galleries reviewed by the National Audit Office have shops and mail order arrangements. And all but the National Portrait Gallery have catering outlets and they have plans for restaurant facilities after the current Development Plan and when finance becomes available. With the exception of the shops at the National Portrait Gallery and the Natural History Museum, shops and catering outlets are run by trading subsidiaries, contractors or franchisees.

Figure 10: Shops performance 1991–92

	British Museum	National Gallery	National Museum of Science & Industry	National Portrait Gallery	Natural History Museum
Shop Turnover (£000)	3626	2900	1605	335	1361
Gross profit (%)	35	44.1	43	39	46
Net profit (%)	11.5	23.8	8.7	9	5.9
Shop Spend per visitor	67p	65p	61.5p	56p	92p

Source: Institutions' Trading Statements
Note: Institutions' trading figures, particularly turnover, gross and net profit are often prepared on different bases and are therefore not necessarily directly comparable.

Shops

3.40 Financial records showed variations between institutions in the average amounts visitors spent, from 56p to 92p (Figure 10). The marketing consultant engaged by the National Audit Office advised that £1.00 per visitor would be a reasonable industry target for visitor attractions. Of course levels of spend should be seen in the light of the educational objectives of institutions and some research suggests that children in school parties have only 50p to spend. The low financial returns on some operations and the low proportion of visitors making purchases, as shown by the National Audit Office visitor survey, suggested that there were opportunities for significantly improving visitors' satisfaction from this element of their visits, as well as potential for generating additional income.

3.41 The National Audit Office visitor survey showed that a significant number of visitors failed to take advantage of the retail facilities at institutions. On average, only 60 per cent visited a shop, although this proportion fell to around a half at the National Gallery and a third at the National Portrait Gallery (Figure 11). The National Audit Office considered that the latter proportion might have been improved had the exit from the Gallery itself been signposted through the bookshop. New signing is to be installed throughout the Gallery to coincide with the opening of the new galleries in November 1993. We noted that the bookshop closed at 4.45 pm, 15 minutes before the Gallery closed, thereby denying any last minute sales. This was also 75 minutes before the neighbouring National Gallery closed during the week.

3.42 The survey showed that shop visitors were more likely to be from abroad or to be accompanied by children. The predominant reason for not visiting shops was lack of interest in making a purchase. Of those who did visit shops, half spent nothing and a quarter spent less than £5.

Figure 11: Visitors at the shops

Percentages	Total	British Museum	National Gallery	National Portrait Gallery	Natural History Museum*	Science Museum*
Visiting the shop	60	69	51	33	57	65
Spending:						
Nothing	49	46	51	53	33	57
Less than £1	7	6	11	10	2	7
£1 to £4.99	19	18	18	18	31	18
£5 to £9.99	10	10	9	9	14	9
£10+	14	18	10	7	18	9
Don't know	1	2	1	3	2	0

Source: NOP Visitor Survey for NAO prepared May/June 1992
*A charge is made for admission.

Figure 12: Visitors' use of catering facilities

Percentages	Total	British Museum	National Gallery	Natural History Museum	Science Museum
Using	31	26	25	41	44
Not using	69	74	75	59	56

Source: NOP Visitor Survey for NAO prepared May/June 1992

Catering

3.43 The National Audit Office visitor survey showed that about seven out of ten visitors did not use the catering facilities (Figure 12). Reasons for not using the facilities included not being hungry or not having time, with 11 per cent commenting that they looked too expensive. High prices were confirmed by those using the facilities and was the main criticism. Only 18 per cent thought prices were good, while 44 per cent said they were average and around a third said prices were poor (Figure 13). These comments related, in the main, to the less expensive of the institutions' catering facilities where there was a choice, and point to the scope for reviewing the range and price of refreshments offered.

3.44 Although not one of the factors considered by the survey, the National Audit Office noted that credit cards were not accepted at several of the catering facilities. Overseas visitors, in particular, may find this surprising and inconvenient and the catering facilities may as a result lose customers.

3.45 Some museums had recently brought in professional expertise to assist in improving the performance of their retail outlets. The Science Museum had used visitor research and retail consultants to develop a product strategy for its shops. The Natural History Museum had used consultants to assess retail performance. They identified potential for greater profitability and the need for merchandise to be revised to take advantage of unmet requirements of significant visitor groups. The British Museum had reviewed their retailing policy in the 1970s and since then had recruited the appropriate professionals to run their retail outlets.

Figure 13: Visitors' ratings of the catering facilities

Rating of the Catering Facilities	Mean Score	British Museum	National Gallery	Natural History Museum	Science Museum
Cleanliness	0.70	0.64	0.79	0.72	0.68
Layout	0.55	0.49	0.56	0.69	0.54
Product quality	0.54	0.52	0.75	0.46	0.41
Staff service	0.54	0.39	0.75	0.62	0.51
Range of food and drink	0.28	0.32	0.53	0.09	0.12
Prices	−0.17	−0.28	0.18	−0.34	−0.25
Overall Assessment	0.43	0.37	0.64	0.44	0.33

Source: NOP Visitor Survey for NAO prepared May/June 1992.
Scores based on good (+1); average (0); poor (−1).

Part 4: Promotion and publicity

Introduction

4.1 The national museums and galleries are major visitor attractions and researching the aspirations, expectations and needs of visitors and potential visitors or audiences and then designing or adapting services so as to enhance visitors' satisfaction is relevant to a substantial part of the activities of museums and galleries. So is monitoring the experiences of visitors so as to inform the planning processes that maintain and extend quality of service. The institutions examined told the National Audit Office that they each have a number of different audiences with different perceptions, and that promotional activities usefully portray different images to different types of visitor, such as foreign visitors, school groups or local residents.

4.2 At the Natural History Museum and the Science Museum professional marketing activities had expanded rapidly since the late 1980s when admission charges were introduced. This was in part to generate income by providing the right sort and quality of services and attractions.

The UK visitor attraction market

4.3 To set the museums and galleries in the visitor attractions context, a survey by the British Tourist Authority and the English Tourist Board ('Sightseeing in the UK 1991') showed that of the 5,188 listed tourist attractions in the UK, 1,669 were museums or art galleries, an increase of 570 since 1970. Nearly 345 million visits to tourist attractions were recorded in 1991, some 77 million to museums and galleries of which 20 million were to the eleven national museums and galleries funded by the Department. Figure 14 shows that the British Museum, the National Gallery, the Natural History Museum and the Science Museum were among the most visited UK museums and galleries in 1991. Notably, the Science Museum in London and the Natural History Museum sustained or increased their visitor numbers at a time when visitor numbers at other charging attractions in the UK were declining. The British Museum and the National Gallery had very significantly increased visitor numbers in 1991.

Figure 14: Most visited Museums and Galleries in the UK

Ranking		1991 Visits
1	British Museum, London	5,061,000
2	National Gallery, London	4,280,000
3	Tate Gallery, London	1,816,000
4	Natural History Museum, London	1,500,000
5	Science Museum, London	1,328,000
6	Victoria and Albert Museum, London	1,066,000
7	Glasgow Art Gallery and Museum	893,000
8	Royal Academy, London	808,000
9	Jorvik Viking Centre, York	791,000
10	Birmingham Museum and Art Gallery	754,000
11	National Museum of Photography, Film and Television, Bradford	711,000
12	Castle Museum, Nottingham	695,000
13	Tate Gallery, Liverpool	597,000
14	National Portrait Gallery, London	590,000
15	National Maritime Museum, London	588,000

Source: Visits to Tourist Attractions 1991 British Tourist Authority/English Tourist Board May 1992

4.4 Against this background the National Audit Office examined who visited the national museums and galleries and why. They also examined the extent of promotional activities and the evaluation by the institutions of the impact and effectiveness of such activities.

Visitor profile

4.5 Paragraph 3.11 describes the extent of visitor research by the institutions. Only the Science and the Natural History museums carried out regular surveys to build a demographic profile of visitors and to assess their attitudes and levels of satisfaction. Survey information was supplemented by data resulting from charging for admission. The surveys had concentrated on exhibitions and displays. These two museums had also researched non-visitors to ascertain what misconceptions, apprehensions or prejudices inhibit their potential audiences, for example, limited perceptions of museums and science. The Science Museum subsequently ran an advertising campaign specifically to change some of the common perceptions.

4.6 The National Audit Office survey (Figure 15) showed that three out of five respondents were first time visitors. Just under half were resident in the United Kingdom and a quarter were from North America. About 94 per cent of the visitors were from the ABC social classes which compares to 68 per cent of the

population as a whole. Some 56 per cent of visitors were over 35 years of age. Except for estimates of the numbers of educational groups by some national museums and galleries, they do not set sectional targets for visitor groups. Some institutions told the National Audit Office that they expected the emphasis upon school groups to redress, in time, the social mix of adult visitors.

4.7 Overall, 43 per cent of visits were to see a specific exhibition or part of the collection, and the rest were of a general nature. Less than 5 per cent of the visitors surveyed took advantage of the more specialised seminars, lectures and guided tours offered.

Marketing plans

4.8 The National Audit Office examined the five institutions' marketing plans and reviewed their marketing objectives, visitor research programmes, identification of target audiences and visitor groups and promotion and publicity activities. They also reviewed mechanisms for monitoring and review of marketing activities including the setting of performance targets or other quantitative measures of success. They found that the Natural History Museum had prepared the most detailed and comprehensive marketing planning documents of the five institutions examined. Their Department of Commerce and Marketing's Strategic Plan had been prepared in April 1992. The Department of

Figure 15: Profile of Adult Visitors

Percentage of Visitors	Total	British Museum	National Gallery	National Portrait Gallery	Natural History Museum	Science Museum
First time visitors	61	61	55	55	65	70
UK Residents	46	33	48	62	63	54
North American Residents	24	36	23	19	11	13
One visitor in party	37	34	48	52	25	31
Two visitors in party	40	41	40	41	46	37
Visitors accompanied by children	14	9	4	1	42	32
Social Class						
AB Professional, Manager	45	49	42	53	34	44
C1 Office Workers, Junior Professions	41	35	46	36	50	38
C2 Skilled Manual	8	9	5	7	10	12
DE Unskilled, Retired	6	7	7	4	6	6
Aged under 35	44	38	46	41	54	48
Aged 35-54	37	40	32	30	36	38
Aged 55 and over	19	22	22	29	10	14
Male	52	52	46	45	51	65
Female	48	48	54	55	49	35

Source: NOP Visitor Survey prepared for NAO May/June 1992

National Heritage told the National Audit Office that as with any other aspect of management, were the museums and galleries together to suggest that a common initiative on marketing strategies could be of benefit, the Department would consider how they could help.

Promotional activity

4.9 The National Audit Office found extensive activity at all the institutions to promote themselves and to provide information on their collections, services and facilities. And there were other activities which, as by-products, promoted interest in the institutions. These included:

- creation of new exhibitions and displays;

- hosting temporary exhibitions, many of which are sponsored;

- hospitality, press launches and press releases for events such as the opening of a new exhibition, to generate free press, radio and television coverage;

- paid advertising using selected media and posters sited mainly in London and including Underground sites. The Natural History Museum also advertised on the sides of London buses. The National Museum of Science and Industry advertised locally for its York and Bradford attractions and used paid television and radio advertising. Professional advertising agencies are used by all of the institutions, except the National Portrait Gallery, to advise on methodology and design and to carry out advertising campaigns;

- publications, ranging from scholarly works to guidebooks, help widen access to the collections and disseminate scholarly and research work and indirectly promote museums and galleries. The British Museum and the National Gallery have the most extensive publications programmes with worldwide distribution;

- mail order arrangements primarily generate income but also project the institutions more generally. The National Gallery sell products internationally and the National Railway Museum has a strong mail-order base in Japan;

- leaflets and brochures were in some cases carried at other galleries and at tourist offices, libraries and, in the cases of the National Gallery and the National Portrait Gallery, were distributed to schools, colleges, hotels and businesses;

- entries, usually free, in tourist guidebooks;

- promotions and advertising run jointly with other organisations, for example the National Railway Museum with British Rail and other attractions in York. The National Portrait Gallery had undertaken a joint promotion with the National Theatre. The Natural History Museum had promotions on the packaging of products such as Flora margarine and Royal Mail stamps.

4.10 The National Audit Office noted there had been significant successes in developing product licensing, royalties and merchandising whereby institutions endorse products with subject matter associated with their collections. Some also sell the rights to images of items in the collections for commercial uses. This not only generates income but gives world-wide publicity to the institutions involved. For example, the Natural History Museum had received over £300,000 in 1990–91 from licensing, endorsements and third party promotions from such diverse items as model dinosaurs, table mats and a licensed "Natural History Book of Trees".

4.11 Of the institutions examined, only the National Museum of Science and Industry had run advertising and promotional campaigns specially targeted at discrete groups. Sixteen such campaigns were run in 1991–92. Measurable targets had been set for these campaigns and their impacts were reviewed. The Natural History Museum in their 1992 plans identified key audiences and the messages they wished to promote, although specific promotional campaigns had not been developed at the time of the National Audit Office study.

Promotional and marketing expenditure

4.12 Management need to have a measure of the cost of their marketing activities in order to gauge their cost effectiveness and to inform decisions on priorities between general and specific promotional campaigns. The National Audit Office found that the Science Museum and the Natural History Museum had budget and accounting structures capable of routinely identifying and monitoring their total promotional, advertising and marketing costs. And other institutions could identify particular cost elements. Staff costs consumed by marketing and promotional activities were not aways identifiable as staff were often not exclusively employed in marketing tasks and no institution operated a time recording system to collect the relevant staff costs. In the absence of common definitions of marketing, public relations and publicity activities and collection of appropriate costs, comparison between institutions is difficult. However, marketing at the five institutions cost in excess of £2 million a year and is likely to be nearer £3 million a year if staff costs are included.

Monitoring and review of marketing activities

4.13 Institutions had not defined targets or success criteria for evaluation of the success of marketing or promotional expenditure. Monitoring consisted largely of collecting records of press and media coverage, visitor surveys, visitor numbers and figures for self-generated income. The trend in visitor attendances over the last five years is shown at Appendix 6 with the number of visits overall remaining at about 21 million. Individual institutions showed marked fluctuations, for some partly related to the introduction of admission charges; for others related to major new attractions.

4.14 Of the institutions examined, only the Natural History Museum and the National Museum of Science and Industry had carried out sufficient research to facilitate an annual assessment of the impact of their marketing activities on different visitor groups and on customer satisfaction. Some other institutions carried out surveys in connection with major exhibitions which allowed some assessment of specific marketing impacts. The Science Museum was the only institution to have formally assessed the effectiveness of its advertising. Market research at the Science Museum in 1989 and 1990, using structured questionnaires, ascertained the awareness of the Science Museum's advertising amongst the London public. This showed that awareness had risen from 8 per cent in 1989 to 15 per cent in 1990 and that the advertising had a positive effect on the attitude of the public towards the Museum. The Natural History Museum have introduced "effectiveness of advertising" as a performance indicator for 1992–93 and work is in hand to quantify this.

4.15 Figure 16 shows the results of the National Audit Office survey for the impact of advertising and publicity on visitors. Some 10 per cent of visitors were prompted to visit by advertising and publicity, which is considered a good response in the marketing industry. The institutions pointed out that their high international profile contributed a great deal to the sustained level of overseas visitors. The National Audit Office survey suggested that the biggest single prompt to visit was word of mouth (19 per cent) followed by tourist information and guidebooks (15 per cent). The highest response was at the Natural History Museum where 23 per cent of the visitors surveyed had been prompted to visit by the advertising and publicity, probably reflecting the publicity for the "Dinosaurs" exhibition which had recently opened. The Science

Figure 16: Responses to advertising and publicity

Percentage response rate to:	British Museum	National Gallery	National Portrait Gallery	Natural History Museum	Science Museum	Average at all institutions
Posters	2	2	3	3	1	2
Newspaper/magazine	7	2	6	13	1	5
TV/Radio	1	1	—	6	—	2
Leaflet	1	1	3	1	2	1
Total	11	6	12	23	4	10

Source: NOP Visitor Survey Prepared for NAO May/June 1992

Museum considered that their low response rate to advertising was because they had not advertised for some six months prior to the visitor survey. The National Portrait Gallery did not have posters on public display around the time of the survey although 3 per cent of their visitors remembered them. In general, the Science Museum's marketing activities are recognised within the marketing industry to be of a very high quality and have won several awards including that of the trade magazine 'Campaign' in 1991 for the most effective poster advertising.

Appendix 1
Outline of roles of selected National Museums and Galleries

	British Museum	National Gallery
Scope of Collections	Worldwide human history and culture	Western European painting 13th to early 20th Century
Fundamental aims or mission	to hold in trust for the nation and in perpetuity those parts of the national collections given to its care	preserving, caring for and adding to the national collection; and enabling access by the public who are its owners
Public Services	— 113 permanent galleries at British Museum and Museum of Mankind — temporary exhibitions (16 new in 1991–92) — c2,800 objects loaned to other exhibitions — education service providing advice, materials, teaching — public lectures/gallery talks/films — guided tours — information/enquiry/advisory service — publications — shops — cafes and restaurant — British Museum Tours to historic sites — student rooms — photographic services	— free display of whole available collection — 2–3 major charging exhibitions and about 4 smaller exhibitions a year — loans to other exhibitions — education service providing direct teaching, free public lectures, films, guided tours, study days, teachers courses — information service, access to libraries — publications and videos — shops — restaurants — Micro Gallery interactive computer system — seminar/conference rooms — photographic services
Running Cost Budget 1992–93 (£ million)	26.7	13.2
Approximate staff numbers	1,100	410

* Museum makes admission charges

National Portrait Gallery	Natural History Museum(*)	Science Museum(*)
Portraits of people prominent in British history and culture	Worldwide biological and geological specimens and drawings	History of science, technology, industry and medicine
to promote the appreciation and understanding of the men and women who have made and are making British history and culture, and to stimulate the general understanding of British history and culture through the medium of portraits; and to promote the appreciation and understanding of the art of portraiture in all media.	to promote the understanding and enjoyment of the variety of the natural world through high quality exhibitions, education and science	to be the nation's leading centre for the public understanding of science by caring for, presenting and interpreting the national collections of science, technology and medicine
— free display of collection at National Portrait Gallery	— exhibitions at museum: Life and Earth Galleries	— 3 major museums: Science Museum National Railway Museum National Museum of Photography, Film and Television
— outstations at stately homes in Somerset, Lancashire, Yorkshire, Clwyd	— education service including Resource Centre for teachers, lectures, children's tours, field study	— temporary exhibitions (25 in 1991–92)
— about 7 exhibitions per year, some charging	— permanent and touring Discovery Centre	— guides, explainers in galleries, information
— education service for schools and adults, free public lectures	— guides, information	— free educational visits, interactive galleries
— picture library	— free access to library	— gallery drama
— free access to collections, archive, library for research	— publications	— library and information enquiry service
— publications	— shops	— publications
— shop	— restaurants	— shops
		— cafe
3.9	30.6	21.5
120	720	446

Appendix 2
Performance Indicators

Group 1: For Department and institutional use and required to be included in Annual Corporate Plans

Summary

Performance Component	Indicator Area
Access and Use	Movement in user numbers by category eg. school parties
Access and Use	Expenditure per user
Access and Use	New loans made from the collections
Visitor Care/Display	Visitor satisfaction measured by independent opinion poll
Visitor Care/Display	Gallery days: availability vs plan
Display	Achievement of display programme objective (institution specifies)
Access/Display/ Visitor Care	Visitor flow — ratio of highest to lowest monthly visitor numbers
Collection Management	Achievement of specified collection management objectives for Corporate Planning period
Collection Management/ Scholarship	Views of assessors
Scholarship	Scholarly outputs vs plan
Scholarship	Citations/critical review/other impact assessment
Building Management	Major projects: variance in actual time and cost vs plan
Building Management	Ratio of planned to unplanned maintenance
Building Management	Compliance with fire standards
Building Management	Accident levels
Income Generation and Financial Management	Increase in self-generated income by type
Income Generation and Financial Management	Ratio of self-generated income to grant-in-aid
Income Generation and Financial Management	Salaries as percentage of running costs grant-in-aid
Human Resource Management	Achievement of training programme objectives

Source: Coopers and Lybrand report to the Office of Arts and Libraries in 1991.

Appendix 3
Performance Indicators

Group 2: For institutional use, without being disclosed to the Department

Summary

Performance Component	Indicator Area
Visitor Care	Number of complaints by type/service area per 1,000 visitors
Visitor Care	Gallery equipment downtime vs standard eg. interactive facilities
Visitor Care	Other amenities: downtime and quality standards eg. lavatories
Visitor Care/Human Resource Management	Staff resources available vs plan
Visitor Care/Human Resource Management	Individual exhibitions: visitor enjoyment and understanding measured by market research
Visitor Care/Human Resource Management	Increase/decrease in display space available
Visitor Care/Human Resource Management	Percentage available display space not used for display purposes
Scholarship	Staff qualifications eg. percentage staff with academic and professional qualifications
Scholarship	Research grant and other income
Scholarship	Publication sales volumes
Building Management	Minor projects: variance in actual time and cost vs plan
Building Management	Management cost per square metre as a percentage of total building spend
Building Management	Total Maintenance costs per square metre
Income Generation and Financial Management	Admission income per visitor
Income Generation and Financial Management	Sales per square metre of trading operations
Human Resource Management	Staff turnover by grade and function
Human Resource Management	Movement in average age of staff by grade
Human Resource Management	Average sickness days per staff member by grade and function
Human Resource Management	Movement of staff to external developmental posts in other institutions/bodies

Source: Coopers and Lybrand report to the Office of Arts and Libraries in 1991

Appendix 4
Public facilities and services at the selected National Museums and Galleries

	British Museum	National Gallery	National Portrait Gallery	Natural History Museum	Science Museum
Information leaflet	Yes	Yes	Yes	Yes	Yes
Floor plan	Yes	Yes	Yes	Yes	Yes
Information desk	Yes (2)	Yes (2)	Yes	Yes	Yes
Guided tours	2–4 per day*	2–5 per day	August only	occasional	2 per day
Audio tour	Elgin Marbles only*	Exhibitions only*	No	No	No
Foreign language provision	Guidebooks	Guidebooks	No	No	Guidebooks
Shops	4–7	3	1	6	2
Cafe/restaurant	3	2	No	3	2
Cloakroom	Yes	Yes	Yes	Yes	Yes
Disabled access	Yes but not all areas accessible	Yes	Special entrance arrangements needed	Special entrance arrangements needed	Yes but not all areas accessible
Baby changing facilities	Yes	Yes	No	Yes	Yes
Schools education	Access and materials for classes; some taught groups	Taught groups; worksheets etc	Taught groups	Resources/advice for teachers; Discovery Centre (touring)	Resources for teachers; interactive galleries
Children's events	Drama, music, holiday events	Holiday events	Holiday events	Children's tours	Gallery drama & demonstrations
Lectures	2 per day	5+ per week	6 per week	occasional	occasional
Other special events	Films; study days*; open evenings*	Films; study days*	Films/videos	Field study tours*; videos	Films, demonstrations
Access to reserve collection	Yes	Yes	Yes	Yes	Yes
Access to other information	Student rooms (Depts' exhibits and libraries); advice on finds; identification service	Micro Gallery; library; picture vetting	Library and archive; picture library*	Library; access to databases*	Library; Information Service for students

* Fee charged

Appendix 5
NOP visitor questionnaire

Note: Not all the questions asked at institutions gave comparable or statistically significant results. In these cases, tables of results are not shown.

NOP visitor survey of Museums and Galleries: questionnaire and summary results

Name: (Mr/Mrs/Miss) _____

Address: _____

_____

_____ Tel No. (incl STD code)

ESTABLISH WHETHER HEAD OF HOUSEHOLD IS: (READ OUT AND CIRCLE)

Working (either full or part-time) 1   GIVE DETAILS BELOW OF
Retired or not working with PRIVATE PENSIONS/MEANS 2   PRESENT OR LAST
Unemployed less than 2 months 3   OCCUPATION

Unemployed over 2 months 4   ASK IF THERE IS ANY CHIEF WAGE EARNER
Retired with STATE BENEFIT/PENSION only 5   IN THE HOUSEHOLD. IF YES, ASK OCCUPATION
Not working with STATE BENEFIT only 6   IF NO CODE E'

Student 7

TICK WHETHER OCCUPATION IS THAT OF .... Head of Household .... or Chief Wage Earner ....

Job Title _____

Job Description _____

Industry _____ Size of Company _____

Qualifications _____

If Manager/Supervisor/Self-Employed, Number of People Responsible for: _____

Analysis of Visitors

SOCIAL CLASS

PERCENTAGE VISITORS	
AB	45
C1	40
C2	8
DE	7

SEX

PERCENTAGE VISITORS	
Male	52
Female	48

AGE

Mean Age	39.6

AGE	PERCENTAGE VISITORS
15–34	44
35–54	37
55+	19

NORMAL PLACE OF RESIDENCE

PERCENTAGE VISITORS	
UK	46
Europe	17
North America	24
Other	13

CHILDREN UNDER 16	PERCENTAGE VISITORS
One	7
Two	4
Three or More	3

PARTY SIZE

Q. How many people are there, including yourself, in your immediate party today?

PARTY SIZE	PERCENTAGE VISITORS
Self Only	37
Two	40
Three	9
Four	6
Five or More	7
Don't Know	1

Mean Party Size	2.5

Q. And how many of them are children (aged under 16)?

Visitors with Children	14%

Screening question:

QA. Can I just check, have you looked around the museum/gallery today or did you come here purely for research or to visit the library?

Looked around museum/gallery ....

Research/library only* ....

* No further questions were asked at this group.

Detailed questions:

Q1. Including today's visit, how many times have you visited this museum/gallery in the last two years?

PERCENTAGE VISITORS	
Once	61
Regularly (2–3 times)	18
Frequently (4–8 times)	9
Very often (9+ times)	10
Can't remember	2

Q2. *SHOWCARD A* Did any of the following prompt you to visit the museum/gallery today?

PERCENTAGE VISITORS		
ADVERT:	Underground poster	2
	Newspaper/magazine	3
	TV/Radio	1
PUBLICITY:	TV/Radio	1
	Newspaper/magazine	2
	Leaflet	1
	Tourist information/guide book	15
OTHER:	Passing door	7
	Word of mouth	19
	Organised trip	3
	Other	21
	None of these	25
	Don't know	7

Multiple answers were allowed.

ASK ALL

Q3. How long did you expect your visit to take today?

Q4. And how long did your visit actually take today?

PERCENTAGE VISITORS	EXPECTED LENGTH OF VISIT	ACTUAL LENGTH OF VISIT
Less than half an hour	7	7
Half an hour to 1 hour	19	16
Over 1 hour, up to 2 hours	35	36
Over 2 hours, up to 3 hours	17	22
Over 3 hours	15	17
Don't know	7	2

PERCENTAGE VISITORS	
Visit shorter than expected	10
Visit same length as expected	62
Visit longer than expected	21
Don't know	7

Q5a. Which of the following did you collect or buy at the museum/gallery?

Q5b. Of the remainder, which would you have liked?

PERCENTAGE VISITORS	Bought/ Collected	Would have liked
A free floor plan	60	9
A programme of events	12	11
Guided tour information	4	8
Audio guide or recorded tour	*	4
Guide book	8	12
(None of these)	35	66

* less than 0.5%
Multiple answers were allowed.

ASK ALL

Q6. To help you find your way around the gallery/museum did you do any of the following?

Q7. How helpful did you find them?

PERCENTAGE VISITORS	Usage	Helpfulness				
		1	2	3	4	5
Use the floor plan	57	60	33	6	1	0
Look at the information boards	57	50	41	7	1	1
Follow signposting	65	48	39	10	2	1
Buy a guide book	7	36	29	17	6	12
Ask staff	33	83	13	2	1	1
None of these	11	—	—	—	—	—

1 = Very helpful
2 = Helpful
3 = Not very helpful
4 = Not at all helpful
5 = Don't know

Q8. Overall, how easy was it to find your way around the museum/gallery?

PERCENTAGE VISITORS	
Very easy	42
Easy	37
Neither easy nor difficult	14
Difficult	6
Very difficult	1

Q9. Was today's visit a general visit or did you come to see something in particular?

PERCENTAGE VISITORS	
General visit	57
Something in particular	43

Q10. If something in particular did you have any of the following in mind?

A special or new exhibition?

Permanent exhibitions

Seminar or lecture

Film/video shows

Expert advice from staff

Shop

Restaurant

Other

Note:
Amalgamation of results from individual institutions would not be meaningful

Q11a. Which of the following features did you see or make use of today?

PERCENTAGE VISITORS USED	
Seminar or lecture	3
Film/video shows	12
Expert advice from staff/information desk	5
Guided tour	3
None of these	79

Multiple answers were allowed.

Q11b. How would you rate them?
Note: Ratings not statistically significant.

Q12. Which of these displays have you seen?

Q13. Which display did you like *most*?

Q14. And which display did you like *least*?

NB: Different at each institution. Science Museum results shown as an example below.

PERCENTAGE VISITORS	Q12 Seen	Q13 Most Liked	Q14 Least Liked
A. Science and art of medicine	35	6	2
B. Glimpses of medical history	28	6	1
C. Flight lab	55	8	2
D. Aeronautics	54	8	4
E. Geophysics and oceanography	21	*	2
F. Radio, photography and cinematography	36	2	2
G. Chemistry, nuclear physics and power	35	4	4
H. Computing	42	3	6
I. Ships and navigation	47	8	4
J. Agriculture	30	1	3
K. Food for thought	37	2	2
L. Launch pad	49	12	1
M. Meteorology, time measurement and surveying	32	2	1
N. Power	39	2	1
O. The exploration of space	67	15	2
P. Walking through space exhibition	54	4	2
Q. Land transport	53	8	3
R. Firefighting	38	*	1
S. Children's gallery	24	2	*
T. Domestic appliances	18	1	1
U. Firemaking	14	*	1
Not stated	1	8	55

* Less than 0.5%
Multiple answers were allowed.

Q15. How would you rate the following aspects of the display you liked *most*?

PERCENTAGE VISITORS	Rated Good	Rated Average	Rated Poor	Don't Know
The general layout	86	12	2	0
The general presentation	90	9	*	1
Space to view	81	15	3	1
Heating	58	21	18	3
Lighting	85	10	4	1
Cleanliness	95	4	*	1

* less than 0.5%

Q16. How would you rate the following aspects of the display you liked *least*?

PERCENTAGE VISITORS	Rated Good	Rated Average	Rated Poor	Don't Know
The general layout	51	25	10	14
The general presentation	52	25	10	13
Space to view	62	19	7	12
Heating	50	21	15	14
Lighting	67	17	4	12
Cleanliness	81	7	*	12

* Less than 0.5%

Q17. How would you rate the *labelling* of the displays/pictures in general?

PERCENTAGE VISITORS	
Good	71
Average	16
Poor	10
Don't Know	3

Q18. Overall, how satisfied were you with the following at this museum/gallery?

PERCENTAGE VISITORS	Very satisfied	Fairly satisfied	Neither	Fairly dissatisfied	Very dissatisfied	Don't know	Didn't use
The staff	53	16	4	*	*	5	22
Seating	33	23	9	9	2	4	20
Toilets	40	17	3	2	1	1	36
Cloakrooms	15	5	1	1	1	2	75
Opening hours	49	27	5	7	1	9	2

* Less than 0.5%

Q19. Thinking about all the displays you have seen today, how satisfied were you overall?

PERCENTAGE VISITORS	
Very satisfied	74
Fairly satisfied	23
Neither	1
Fairly dissatisfied	1
Very dissatisfied	0
Don't know	1

Q20. Did anything you have seen during your visit today make you want to find out more about that subject?

PERCENTAGE VISITORS	
Yes	61
No	33
Don't Know	6

Q21. Now I would like you to think about some of the other facilities provided. Did you use any of the catering facilities?

PERCENTAGE VISITORS	
Yes	31
No	69

Q22. If not why didn't you use any of the catering facilities?

PERCENTAGE VISITORS	
(Perceived) too expensive	11
(Perceived) too crowded	3
Not thirsty/hungry	34
Wrong time of day	10
No time	21
Did not like last time	*
Changed mind	*
Closed	1
Other	13
Don't know	7

* Less than 0.5%

Q23. How would you rate each of the following at the catering facility(ies)?

PERCENTAGE VISITORS	Rated Good	Rated Average	Rated Poor	Don't Know
Range of food and drink	41	38	15	6
Prices	18	44	34	4
Product quality	58	31	6	5
Staff service	58	31	6	5
Cleanliness	73	22	4	1
Layout	63	26	9	2
Overall assessment	50	39	8	3

Q24. Did you visit the museum/gallery shop?

PERCENTAGE VISITORS	
Yes	60
No	39
Don't Know	1

Q25. If not, why didn't you go into the shop?

(Perceived) too expensive
(Perceived) too crowded
Not enough time
Changed mind
Closed
Did not like it last time
Not interested
Other
Don't know

Note:
Amalgamation of results at individual institutions would not be meaningful

Q26a. How would you rate each of the following at the shop(s)?

PERCENTAGE VISITORS	Rated Good	Rated Average	Rated Poor	Don't Know
Range of goods	62	29	5	4
Prices	20	44	16	20
Quality of goods	72	18	2	8
Staff service	46	15	3	36
Cleanliness	88	8	*	4
Layout	67	25	4	4
Overall assessment	63	31	2	4

* Less than 0.5%

Q26b. How much did you spend?

PERCENTAGE VISITORS	
Spent Nothing	49
Less than £1	7
£1 to £4.99	19
£5 to £9.99	10
£10+	14
Don't know	1

Q27. Overall, how satisfied were you with your visit to the museum/gallery today?

PERCENTAGE VISITORS	
Very satisfied	78
Fairly satisfied	20
Neither satisfied nor dissatisfied	1
Fairly dissatisfied	1
Very dissatisfied	*
Don't know	*

* Less than 0.5%

Q28. How likely are you to visit this museum/gallery again in the next two years?

PERCENTAGE VISITORS	
Very likely	55
Fairly likely	21
Not very likely	11
Not at all likely	9
Don't know	4

Appendix 6
Admission statistics for the National Museums and Galleries funded by the Department of National Heritage 1987 to 1993

	(Thousand Visitors)						
	1987 Actual	1988 Actual	1989 Actual	1990 Actual	1991 Actual	1992 Estimated	1993 Projected
British Museum	4,008	4,172	4,686	5,100	5,410	6,725	6,750
Natural History Museum	1,999	1,671	1,550	1,594	1,572	1,612	1,450
Imperial War Museum	1,185	1,087	1,212	1,257	1,045	1,141	1,200
National Gallery	3,600	3,200	3,400	3,700	4,300	4,300	3,800
National Maritime Museum	422	670	422	541	594	532	504
National Museums and Galleries on Merseyside	1,329	1,564	1,341	1,293	1,242	1,207	1,220
National Portrait Gallery	733	826	854	826	823	796	850
National Museum of Science and Industry	4,733	3,861	2,608	2,683	2,525	2,579	2,600
Tate Gallery	1,742	2,091	1,940	2,210	1,646	2,151	2,300
Victoria and Albert Museum	1,305	1,329	1,242	1,204	1,348	1,526	1,526
Wallace Collection	168	157	129	136	140	200	205
Total	21,224	20,628	19,384	20,544	20,645	22,769	22,405

Source: Department of National Heritage Annual Report 1993
Note: Statistics include admissions at National Museums' and Galleries' outstations.

Reports by the Comptroller and Auditor General Session 1992-93

The Comptroller and Auditor General has to date, in Session 1992–93, presented to the House of Commons the following reports under Section 9 of the National Audit Act, 1983:

Printed in the United Kingdom for HMSO
Dd 5061907 C1 1/94 51.0.0 56219 ON 273721